Dear John,
Some views for you
painting. have a very
Happy Birthday
from + xx.

Journey Through the British Isles

Harry Cory Wright
Foreword by Adam Nicolson

Journey Through the British Isles

LONDON · NEW YORK

Contents

Foreword by *Adam Nicolson*

As I write this, it is still the last weeks of winter. Although some of the honeysuckles have just leafed up, and there are primroses out on the banks of the lane, there is scarcely a hint of green on the trees, and the wood remains wintry and reserved, a growing world still protecting itself against the possibility of late frost. But here, on the table in front of me, surrounded by Harry's photographs, I have two things: a large bowl of 'Paper White' narcissi, their flower heads as rich and deep a white as any flower can be, and as graceful as they would be in the wild, pumping a sweet, spiced scent into the air around them; and beside them, their companions and opposites, a bunch of radishes, the first of the year, still with specks of soil on them from where they came out of the ground this morning, rooty, earthy, sharp, stumpy little things, tangy, not quite woody but verging on the edge of that, crimson, half-mineral, crunchy and peppery hot.

This may be a slightly sideways approach to a book of landscape photographs, but it seems to me that this pairing, the rooted deliciousness of the radish and the half-etherealized smell of the narcissus blowing across the room towards you, this combination of the earthy and the not-quite-worldly, is in fact just the combination of things on which the beauty of the landscape relies. The landscape is always beautiful because it is the real thing, the earthed reality; and it is always beautiful because it contains within itself the possibilities of a fineness that goes beyond the everyday facts. Either of those terms without the other would not be quite enough. Too much emphasis on the purity of spring flowers, or on the cloddy realities of what is happening in and on the ground – both would be a diminution. The miracle of the landscape, the way in which it can continue to provide soul food for millions of people, depends on the way it manages to produce year in and year out both the bite of the radish and the purity of the narcissus, both the deep and the fine, both the transient and what feels at times like the everlasting.

The journey through Britain that Harry made from the spring equinox to the autumn equinox of 2006 was, as it now appears from his photographs, an evolving response to that double fact about the landscape. It was not about tracing a continuous line round the British Isles.

It was not, in other words, the Tour de Britain, more a mission – and that is a Harry-ish word – to find a necklace of radiantly beautiful places buried within the various landscapes of the country. It was not about miles covered, and not really about capturing views. The whole point of the way he did it, with his camping equipment, his van, his portable oven, was that he could land and dwell and settle in the places he found, in those particular places that seemed to glow with a lit significance, which could produce for him the scent of the soil. His task was to make himself as absorbent as he could be, alert to every nuance, looking for the richer underlying meaning that can be found everywhere, for that combination of earthiness with something more than earthiness, for something that goes beyond the ordinary or perhaps even the material.

As you turn the pages of this book, you will see and feel a two-part transformation rippling through its pages. There is, first, the colour. It begins in ice-blue and the patterning of white snow on black rock, moves on into the damp and serious, almost taciturn, colours of a northern landscape on the edge of winter, on the edge it seems of an ice age that has ended not that long ago; then deepens into green, into the lush of May, that colour that is as rich with desire as any in the universe. 'No white nor red was ever seen', Andrew Marvell wrote in 'The Garden', 'So amorous as this lovely green.' Of course, to most minds, white and red – the colours of flesh and kisses – are the colours of amorousness. But this other green is the colour, if one can say this, of the world's desire, of amorousness on a planetary scale, far beyond the claims of flesh and kisses, the pulse of life itself, the annual thickening of the biosphere, the breeding and seeding that is the source of all natural beauty.

From that springtime ecstasy, the journey moves on and deepens. The green becomes freckled, turns pale in the chalklands of southern England and misty, before high summer starts to make its claims and the colours go tawny, golden and enriched. Only then, as the journey curls north again, do they begin their autumn retreat, moving back towards a careful, closed, winter condition. In a very beautiful and almost subliminal way, the colours in this book describe an orbit, or perhaps half an orbit, of a planet around the sun.

At the same time – and I am sure this was not done programmatically by Harry, but as a response to his own deepening engagement with the landscapes in which he was living, sleeping, walking, smelling and breathing – his relationship to them becomes slowly more intimate. That process, curiously, mimics something of the history of our relationship in this country to landscape beauty. Harry's first, northern pictures are a long way from their subjects. The hard, cold northern lands are seen from high and distant viewpoints. One or two are almost map-like, in the way of the early land surveys, which were the first depictions of landscape in Britain. The point of view moves on and toys with the kind of imagery of which picturesque painters would have approved in the eighteenth and nineteenth centuries, placing important objects carefully in the view, conveying a sense, even in the wild, of orderly hierarchy and the calm arrangement of parts.

But then, as the amorous green floods his world, Harry steps down into a more modern relationship with these places, seeing them very close, or washed by altering and other-worldly light, with an unexpected relationship of parts or the sudden prominence of nothing more than a worn path or a reed-thickened ditch. By the time he has arrived on the banks of the River Wey, his own native place, he has moved on again, dispensing with any sense that these images are in public, that any performance needs to be made, and coming instead to the emotional core of the journey and the book. The photographs on the banks of the Wey make no baroque claims but see intimacy and slightness as the sources of beauty and delicacy – not unimportance – and dwell on the ordinary, the transient and the apparently chaotic as the site of unaffected meaning. That is the still centre of the whole series and Harry's return to the north is shaped by it. Every one of those last big views comes to seem full of the minuscule and the detailed to which our eyes have now become accustomed.

Each of the great journeys through Britain that remain as markers in our collective cultural memory of the landscape carry the impress of their age. During her journeys on horseback in the 1680s, Celia Fiennes tended to notice almost nothing except the very large houses, and their gardens and contents, belonging to the higher gentry of which she was a member. Daniel Defoe recorded the coming of another age in the 1720s, seeing the burgeoning business and industry of a country undergoing its first enormous urban and commercial revolution. William Cobbett's *Rural Rides* (1830) through England a century later focused on the rural victims of that change, the transformation of self-sufficient English yeoman families into impoverished agricultural labourers dependent on the whims of capitalist landlords. By the time J.B. Priestley travelled through England in the 1920s, his journey had become in part a lament for the destruction and pollution of the industrial age and a jealous fear for those parts that remained unaffected by it.

Since then, there has been a deep and pervasive industrialization of the landscape. By 1970, over 9 million acres were being sprayed with weedkiller every year. So much nitrogen had been applied to the fields that it had entered the water cycle, and in some parts of England over 36 pounds of nitrogen would fall on every acre each year in the rain. The average size of a field had increased from 19 acres in 1920 to 45 acres in 1970. The number of farms had halved as agricultural holdings were agglomerated. 'It will be said of this generation', the rural campaigner C.E.M. Joad claimed in 1931, 'that it found England a land of beauty and left it a land of "beauty spots".'

If a photographer had made this journey twenty or thirty years ago, that might have been his burden. Now, though, there is a sense that we have moved on again. There has, without doubt, been a profound degradation of the British landscape. The miracle, however, is that within that landscape there remain many deep reservoirs of beauty and meaning. The wide-ranging, Olympian view is no longer suitable for us or our landscape. What we need to do – perhaps all that we can now do – is make a close engagement with the detail that matters. Intimacy has replaced both the proprietorial survey and the picturesque order that dominated an earlier age. This is what Harry's journey is about: the riches to be found in the hidden corners, in the dust at your feet, in the leaves drifting in a sunlit river, in a daughter swimming for a moment in a summer pond. Here it is; it's everywhere; have a look; minuteness is all.

The beauty of ordinariness, the dazzle and blaze you can sometimes get on an ordinary morning, has for centuries been part of the inherited English tradition, but it is also, I think, an idea that has particular potency at the moment. Gertrude Stein famously said of the suburban anonymity of Oakland, California, that 'There is no there there.' Since then, the gradual erosion of the thereness of there has become one of the most destructive aspects of modern life. As new development absorbs ever more of the country, the appetite for real, rich, beautiful, entrancing places – which are their own middle, the source of their own way of doing things, their own poetry, calm, vitality, whatever it might be – the appetite for such places is on a steep increase.

Places rich with a sense of *there* are what Harry's photography is about. It comes down, essentially, to a new understanding of what is meant by the word 'place'. A place is not just a location. Nor is it an idea or an image. It is intensely concrete, the opposite of anything virtual, something that is thick with its own reality. And, more than that, a place is somewhere with a quality that you might call 'inner connectedness'. That is a subtle but powerful thing, related to a kind of self-sufficiency, a feeling in a place that its life is not borrowed or imposed from elsewhere, but is coming up out of its own soil. It is a rooted and so an organic feeling. It is by definition idiosyncratic, pursuing its own way of doing things, perhaps a little quirkily, not at first entirely easy to understand, but undeniably itself.

Access to those places is not a question of cruising past or sliding by, but more than that, of burrowing in, of taking the landscape and getting under its skin, going feral in it, of blurring the boundaries between yourself and the place. All of that is, to some extent, a retreat from the large-scale claims of the picturesque idea. I would say, though, and the photographs in this book are evidence of it, that a reduction in the scale of the experience brings in its wake a heightening of the intensity. The tighter the focus, the richer the vision. Places have always been the great mnemonics of the culture. People know who they are by the places in which they live. Landscapes enshrine meanings both good and bad, and few forms of record are so permanent. It is true, now, that we have to a large extent driven ourselves back into our precious corners. There is not much meaning or delight in the 100,000 acres of England now covered by motorway. But Harry's journey through this country, over the course of a turning year, has been driven by a belief that in those precious corners, beauty and sustaining meaning are to be found with a significance that is at least as intense as it has ever been.

In one of the *Duino Elegies* (1912–22), as translated here by the American Stephen Mitchell, the German poet Rainer Maria Rilke, hesitantly and modestly but still with an eye on the transcendent, makes the central claim on which a book such as this one is founded:

> But to have been
> This, once, completely, even if only once:
> To have been at one with the earth, seems beyond
> undoing.

Like many of these photographs, those words need reading a few times before their meaning comes through to you. They are not a postcard that flashes an obvious bit of the picturesque in your direction. Instead, carefully but hugely, they make a statement that is both intimate with the earth and unequivocally cosmic in its claims, as pure as the scent of the narcissi on a late winter day. That's what these photographs are, too.

Introduction

It's Wednesday and here I am in the woods, with song thrushes, blackbirds and robins all around me; there are flies humming through the hazel branches and a fragmented light is moving fractionally over the ground as the breeze slips through the bright leaves above. It's 5 o'clock; sort of tea time, but I'm not bothered by that, or all that is usually inferred by this time of day. There is nothing else I should be doing. There is nothing more important now than to write, precisely, and watch these ants crawl over the damp leaves around the base of my tripod, listen to the birds and look at what it is like to be right here in the late afternoon.

24 May, Forest of Dean

I am a photographer, and my job is to bring it all down to no longer than one-fifteenth of a second. Since I was seventeen I have been working in the landscape of the British Isles. I have had many trips, with days of preparation, hours of waiting, moving and thinking, and in the end it all comes down to the moment when I press the shutter and expose the film. The result has always been a series of individual moments of fairly precise engagement with the landscape. The nature of the game has been to reach as deep as you can into the world in front of you and return; it's a sort of hunt, if you like – there's a start and a finish. It's a raid.

So what happens when you extend this approach, give it the shape of a journey, and allow the process of engaging with the landscape to become a thread, with no perceived breaks, where the thrill of taking one picture extends into the process of making the next?

The preparation for such a journey is important and involves a state of mind that I enjoy. I put maps up on the wall and made notes about places that I wanted to visit, all with a keen sense of what the place might look like when I would be there. It was not so much to do with the history of the place but rather the coming together of the time and place, where the weather and time of day were as significant as the location on the map. I soon began to see that the only way to achieve this kind of work would be to stay put in one place for as long as

such a journey round the British Isles would allow. This was to be no tour, no road trip in the true sense of the word, but rather a series of episodes that allowed for a richer response to the land around me. I needed to slow it all down. I needed to take my biggest tripod, the big camera and all the equipment to store these large sheets of film. I needed my van, a trailer to take a few big canvas tents, wooden benches and a set of trestle tables. I needed to create a fundamental base at each place I camped so that the people might come and join me to discuss the place we were in. I needed to bring my family.

I had my eye on a circular journey from the beginning, and I photocopied a series of maps of the British Isles that fitted neatly on to a sheet of A4 paper. Some had complicated routes in thin pencil that darted from one county to the next; stuttering, impossible journeys that left no room for the process to unfold. I can see clearly now the map that we ended up with on the wall before the journey started. We talked about it for many evenings throughout the summer: the route was a simple, slightly imperfect circle, and it was marked with the imprecision of a large marker pen. It started right up north in Shetland and then went down the west coast of Scotland, through Wales and into Cornwall, then through the south of England and up the east coast, crossing over itself somewhere south of the Scottish border and then out into in the Western Isles. Of course, the line turned

The route taken through the British Isles, March to October

Camp at Tilhill, Surrey

Day 116
13 July, 4.49 am
SU 870 441
River Wey, Surrey

out to be wrong, but the nature of it was right. Throughout the journey I was often confused by the important process of studying a map; the exact pinpoint of where a picture had been taken was somehow at odds with the fluid approach of how I got there. This single line of the journey, a flick of the wrist, complete but imprecise and born out of some frustration, I dare say, soon became the key to what we were doing – a talisman to which we would refer many times throughout the summer.

I was clear that I should start in the Shetland Islands and travel south to meet the warmth of the spring. The far north in the month of March was not going to warm my family's spirits to the nature of a six-month trip, so I was to spend the first month alone and meet them on the north-east coast of England in late April.

I started, therefore, on the island of Unst in the Shetland Islands in order to coincide with the spring equinox, and it was cold beyond anything I had imagined possible in the British Isles. The ground became a fragile and brittle skin beneath the scale and drama of snowstorms from the north-west, and I was given only intermittent glimpses of a white and rolling landscape as the clouds cleared. As those dark, leaden clouds broke up, they revealed skies of an intensely fresh blue that I had never noticed before, and I became aware of the possibilities of the task ahead of me. The journey soon became a kind of quest.

There is a state of mind achieved when taking a photograph with the big camera that is both calming and euphoric. It became like a drug, and I soon was obsessed with the idea of keeping alight some sort of fire that had ignited itself during one of those cold, rosy dawns on the Shetland Islands.

To begin with, as I travelled through Scotland, it was all about the majesty of the land and the weather; these were sweeps of land of immense presence, views kept at arm's length. It was only in late May, as the warmth stirred the earth, that I began to take photographs in which I felt the camera became part of the landscape. One morning, at dawn, I walked up a hill behind Lochinver to find a view of Suilven, an unreal-looking mountain to the south-east. It has a shape that dominates any view; you can't take your eyes off it. When I got to the

top the light was flat, but the view was astounding. There was a small valley below with a burn rushing from right to left. On the other side the ground rose steeply through some greenery and then into heather and rocky ground, where it undulated gently like a sea of brown velvet, up and away from me until it reached the base of Suilven itself. I went back for the big camera and spent the afternoon watching the cloud thicken from the west and shape the light on the hills.

Before sunset, as the sun broke through below the cloud, the land lit up like a furnace. The heather at this time of year has the same colours as the Torridonian sandstone – a majestic browny purple that responds to any warm light by appearing to glow with a light from within. I took two photographs of Suilven and then looked to the north, where a shower was passing over the loch below. I put the 10 × 8 in place and exposed the next three sheets in five minutes. It was a view over a small loch, with the landscape stretching way out to the north-east with Quinag in the distance, its peaks cloaked in rain cloud. Some landscape photographs that I take are about being wrapped in a scene, about being a part of it, where the camera is almost the centre of it all. This was not happening here: the clouds, the loch, the trees, the mountains and the sunshine were all part of some fabulous togetherness. I, on the other hand, was a long way away, watching a short moment in a grand world. I packed up as it got dark and then walked back through the trees to the car. It's a good time to walk: the rhythm of your pace, the comfortable weight of the camera and tripod, and the mind taken over by what you've just seen.

I then moved south into Torridon, where the ground is as ancient as it comes. The Torridonian sandstone is sedimentary deposit laid down in waters millions of years ago on top of Lewisian gneiss, a volcanic rock. It's clear for anyone to see the turmoil that has been going on since. There are faults, thrusts and folds where such enormous amounts of time have turned the rocks upside down, and year upon year of erosion has left a land that is shaped by some extraordinary force we can barely imagine. But through the glen one day floated a quality of light so delicate and transient that you somehow felt part of that unfathomable history. It had been changeable weather, with bright sunshine between rich grey clouds of sleet and snow. The cloud rose up from behind the mountains to the north and then spilled over their shoulders into the glen; great soft fingers of mist and rain that seemed to caress the rocky hillsides. It was a powerful world, full of grandeur and the precision of light, and I found a central position and watched it all go off around me.

In the Western Isles it was very different. The weather was overcast, with some dense clouds, rain and a strong wind from the west that got the waves going white and streaky. There were three tones around: the glow through the clouds above; the rich emerald-grey of the sea, with its silvery sheen; and the soft greys of the land of the Uists, North and South. The simplicity of it. I was down from those magnificent hills and out into the Atlantic, where it was damp, fresh and sharp; where the air felt like it had come right out of the water. There was nothing crisp here, not like in the mountains, with those frosts, frozen puddles and everything cold to the touch. This all had salt in it and felt thick, rich and vigorous. It required a different approach to taking the pictures. I had to deal with the sea spray now, with moisture on the lens in the morning, hands that won't dry … and sand.

When a place begins to reveal itself to you, it can come quite slowly. It starts as a response to some central low-key hum from the land, and then grows wider, until you realize that it fits into the frame of the camera. Sometimes it's a question of setting up the camera right there, and I usually find some stone or piece of string to mark the spot while I get the big camera. More often, however, there's a bit of a dance to find exactly the right place to put the tripod. You would think that this is mostly dictated by the composition of the picture, but this is not the case. I remember the beginning of Carlos Castañeda's *Teachings of Don Juan* of 1968 (not my era of enlightenment), in which the author is made to pace around looking for the 'place' where he feels comfortable, where he is at one with himself and the place around him. Something akin to this happens with the plate camera.

Almost always the camera and I find ourselves on some slight ledge, a gentle lift in the land that might just be saying, 'Here's good, have a look from here.' Or is it

perhaps that over thousands of years people have been drawn to witness this place from the same spot and there has grown a deep relationship between view, viewer and place. That is certainly what I feel is going on sometimes: the uniqueness of what you are experiencing is the realization of the moment and the deep sense of being in landscape.

As the warm weather came in May, we stopped in the corner of a field on the banks of the River Tees, where the water flows fast over slippery limestone with a steep cliff on one side and thick woodland on the other. We were among bluebells and wild garlic, where the sunshine was filtered through pale sycamore leaves and alders, and the wood smoke from the fire embedded itself deep into all our clothes. The photographic journey was always as much about times of year and times of day as it was about the specific locations throughout the country – and that week we saw the most spectacular coming together of all the three.

The dawns were warm and glowing with shafts of light through the trees. Mid-morning provided soft shadows on the sandy paths and twisted trunks by the riverside. In the evenings the air became thicker with moisture from the river, showing off the magnificent wholeness of an oak tree, a sycamore and a particular beech by the riverbank. I spent my evenings moving between these three trees with the camera, watching the light soften and round their shapes, provide depth and blend them into the background of the thick woodland behind.

The nights were dominated by the growing moon, which was full the night we left. It rose behind the cliff on the opposite bank, throwing the alder and sycamore branches above us into wonderful twisted silhouettes with a shimmering reflection like black glass on the swirling water beyond. The hot weather began to alter our experience of time, and we all felt a detachment from the outside world, magnified by the separateness of the field, yet we were also thoroughly engaged with the place around us.

We camped in a field again when we got to Cornwall. It was high above the main road from Helston to Penzance. With a gentle breeze from the south you could hear the distant burr of traffic, but it was far enough away to be pleasant. There was much sunshine, and the sea showed us all the variety of blue it could muster; blue-and-pink dawns, bright whites at midday and deep, rich evenings. I travelled a bit to take pictures, but the best came within easy reach. We saw basking sharks in the Helford River, humming-bird hawk moths beside the Camel, speckled woods on the lanes and pathways, and peregrines, swifts, slugs and mullet. But the experience I will most remember was walking at dusk between two fields from Logan's Rock on the south coast. The path has become a deep, sandy lane cut into the land by years of use, with high banks on either side. It was a sunken world: cool, dry, dark and separate from both the earlier heat of the day and the glowing twilight above. Five bats flicked around me, whirring up into the cool air, then skimming over the hedgerow and down into the dark of the lane between the banks of grass and foxgloves. Me and the bats.

Such moments have a completeness, a totality that allows them to be expressed so clearly that they swing quickly to the front of the mind when called. And they carry a strong sense of place; a coming together of time and place. That lane belonged to that shoulder of rock in south-west Cornwall, and the dust I scuffed that rose from the ground, and the air that lingered in the hedgerows that evening were part of it all, as were the stars above us and the camera on my shoulder.

The journey is often defined by its opposites and the implication of the range within: night and day, north and south, fresh water and the sea, travelling and staying still. On the first day in Shetland the brightness of the sunshine had a clarity made more intense by the thick snow clouds and squalls that followed. In Wales I knew that the lush, secluded world beside the Mawddach River was even more beautiful because that morning I had seen the vastness of the surrounding forest from the mountain above. The end of a day only intensifies the dawn that is to follow.

Such range is familiar to us as the year moves through the seasons. We know what it's like when the temperature is -5°F and the wind-chill takes it beyond;

a warm day in July when the temperature is 75°F is a very different day from when it hits 85°F. Throughout the day the swinging combinations of temperature, humidity and the very look of the thing from the angle of the sun throw up these reassurances of where and how we are. During the summer the temperature reached extraordinary record levels in the south of England, and I was on the cliffs at Beachy Head on the South Downs as the highest temperature for a hundred years was being recorded only 25 miles away. It was astonishingly hot, of course, but what I remember most about that hottest hour soon after midday was the completely unfamiliar nature of the sky over the sea. The clouds were expanding rapidly from small cumuli, and the blue had an intensity that belied the hazy nature of the day. The whole thing was moving with a speed that I had never seen before. It was not what I knew; it was an exception, outside the realm of everything that I was working on. It belonged elsewhere.

One warm evening in early July, we went to look for a fish to catch. We padded along the riverbank talking quietly until the light had gone and felt our way back with our hands on the grasses. I returned to the spot with the camera before anyone was awake the next morning, and there was absolute stillness over the water meadows. There was red in the light as the sun rose, and it caught the tops of the tall, curling grass and reeds beside a small brook that leads into the Candover River. It was all so clear, so unique; such a beginning that the sense of prospect was embodied in the light itself. This was the start of a day.

I pushed through the soft mud of the reed beds and set up the camera in cold, knee-deep water, looking upstream through thin mist. It was a moment of intense tranquility, when you wish the camera could do more and drink in the whole morning; gently play back those quiet, liquid sounds of the birds moving in the willows and put out the rich, blended scent of the stirred-up bog and crushed leaves of spearmint.

When I came to photograph the River Wey in Surrey, it was more difficult than I had imagined. The location was a wide meadow down beside the river, full of waving grass and surrounded by oak woods, and through the night it filled with a low-level mist that offered cool relief from the heat of the day. It is a simple, beautiful field, hidden from the busyness of Surrey's network of roads and pathways, and I grew up here.

I learned to fish in the deep pools, catching dace, grayling and perch. I built campfires with my dad here and learned to canoe downriver to meet friends in the village. It has always been the starting place for me, where the world begins; the river coming from somewhere up there, flowing through the field in one great meander and heading off down that way to bigger places that seem quite unimportant. The path down through the wood is where I conquered my deep fear of the dark; it's where I first drank and smoked, where I took my first photographs, and where my father's spirit abounds.

I love this field more than I can describe. To apply the photographic approach that I had been searching for on this journey was not easy. I found myself pointing the camera at familiar spaces, and then began to doubt the relevance to the pictures I had taken so far. As I dug deeper, however, I began to feel that I was perhaps close to finding a kind of key; a sort of secret born out of the quest that I had been on for the last months. I took pictures in the river, among the long grass and in the dappled light under the alders, but the most evocative pictures were taken at dawn as the mist swelled out from the river and cooled over the couple of hundred yards towards the wood. It sat low over the meadow's flatness and moved from one end to the other, almost as if the field were being gently tilted. The mist built up in the stillness, seeping into and over the trees and then, just as the camera was set up and ready, I looked up and it had moved back into the open and was drifting imperceptibly across the field, dragging across the grasses towards the oaks beside the river.

On one afternoon, I remember photographing in the river. I had the tripod set firmly into the gravel on the riverbed and was watching the way the flow of clear water licked the brown edge of the bank and brushed against the tips of the leaves that spilled down the riverbank. My friend Bob Ham came by, and we talked for a while about the warmth, the greenness and the nature

of the place. It struck me that the intensity of his gaze, as he looked down into the river, was how I was looking at everything – or perhaps wanted to look at it: clear, focused and unhurried.

On through the South Downs we encountered those soft dawns that grow quickly into days of flamed July, and we would idle in the shade of canvas throughout the middle of the day. We crossed the Thames with a glance at the metropolis before moving out to the east and to the tidal expanses of north Norfolk. I am familiar with this landscape, and I had wanted one picture that could show the power of the twice-daily flood of tide over salt marsh. Throughout the journey I had begun to concentrate on the effect of the bigger forces of nature on the more intricate elements of landscape, and here, when the big spring tides begin to flood the land, there are moments when you are aware of the full weight of the North Sea behind the waves that roll over the bar, push through the gap and out over the mud-flats of purslane and samphire.

The final leg was up through the spine of England as the air cooled and sweetened towards autumn. I began to round up my thoughts and look at the ways that I could bring this journey to a close with ideas of warm fires and shelter, a sort of homecoming. But when we had drawn on that first map with the thick marker pen, the final kick of the line had passed through the Isle of Skye.

Throughout the journey I had many discussions about the abundance of feelings available when immersed in the British landscape, and we always talked of Loch Coruisk on Skye with a deep reverence. Of all the places I have visited, it is the most like another world – within yet also apart. Surrounded by the mighty Cuillins, you arrive at the grand place – accessible only on foot or by boat – with a sense that you have only just started. It's all just begun; the slate has been wiped clean, and all is well. Such refreshment of spirit is the domain of great landscape.

It has been as thorough and rich a journey as I could have asked for. I look at the photographs that are spread out in front of me as we prepare this book and see that not one of them was taken idly. This was the real thing.

Bob Ham at Tilhill beside the River Wey

Day 118
15 July, 1.11 pm
SU 869 439
River Wey, Surrey

NOTE

Each caption includes the National Grid Reference from which the photograph was taken.

Journey Through the British Isles

Muckle Flugga

Day 1
20 March, 6.44 pm
HP 628 177
Unst, Shetland Islands

Hagdale and the Keen of Hamar

Day 2
21 March, 7.36 am
HP 639 107
Unst, Shetland Islands

Lund

Day 2
21 March, 4.35 pm
HP 576 044
Unst, Shetland Islands

Balta from the Keen of Hamar

Day 3
22 March, 6.27 pm
HP 647 097
Unst, Shetland Islands

Mid Ayre, Uyeasound

Day 4
23 March, 12.01 pm
HP 596 012
Unst, Shetland Islands

Pentland Firth, south-west

Day 7
26 March, 3.49 pm
ND 443 829
Orkney Islands

Pentland Firth, west

Day 7
26 March, 6.19 pm
ND 443 829
Orkney Islands

Towards the Bring Deeps

Day 8
27 March, 5.58 pm
HY 244 091
Orkney Islands

Ben Loyal and Ben Hope

Day 10
29 March, 11.17 am
NC 756 636
Sutherland

The Kyle of Tongue

Day 10
29 March, 7.53 pm
NC 594 590
Sutherland

Suilven

Day 13
1 April, 4.36 pm
NC 107 212
Sutherland

Loch Druim Suardalain and Quinag

Day 13
1 April, 7.43 pm
NC 107 212
Sutherland

West across the Minch

Day 14
2 April, 6.45 pm
NG 741 834
Peterburn, Wester Ross

Above Loch Maree

Day 15
3 April, 10.35 am
NG 998 648
Wester Ross

Torridon

Day 15
3 April, 6.01 pm
NG 895 546
Wester Ross

Neist Point

Day 16
4 April, 7.23 am
NG 130 479
Isle of Skye

Rain cloud over the Outer Hebrides

Day 16
4 April, 10.51 am
NG 129 485
Isle of Skye

Port Scolpaig

Day 20
8 April, 10.33 am
NF 694 702
North Uist

Limestone

Day 26
14 April, 7.40 pm
NM 809 374
Lismore, Argyll and Bute

River Etive

Day 31
19 April, 6.47 pm
NN 208 513
Highland

Mouth of the River Tweed

Day 41
29 April, 7.23 am
NU 006 518
Berwick-upon-Tweed, Northumberland

Berwick-upon-Tweed

Day 43
1 May, 12.54 pm
NT 996 528
Northumberland

High Scawdel above Johnny Wood

Day 46
4 May, 6.41 am
NY 249 159
Borrowdale, Cumbria

Path to Castle Crag

Day 47
5 May, 6.02 pm
NY 249 165
Borrowdale, Cumbria

Beside the Derwent

Day 48
6 May, 11.19 am
NY 259 166
Borrowdale, Cumbria

The pool, Graft's bottom field

Day 50
8 May, 6.14 am
NZ 119 143
Teesdale, County Durham

Beside the River Tees

Day 53
11 May, 9.38 am
NZ 120 147
Teesdale, County Durham

Graft's bottom field

Day 54
12 May, 5.39 pm
NZ 118 144
Teesdale, County Durham

Pendle Hill

Day 60
18 May, 6.25 am
SD 812 420
Lancashire

Gordale Scar

Day 61
19 May, 7.19 pm
SD 915 640
North Yorkshire

Above Settle

Day 62
20 May, 9.38 am
SD 819 652
North Yorkshire

From Worsaw Hill

Day 63
21 May, 7.38 am
SD 778 433
Lancashire

May blossom

Day 69
27 May, 12.08 pm
SO 293 258
Vale of Ewyas, Monmouthshire

Mine pit

Day 67
25 May, 5.34 pm
SO 550 157
Wye Valley, Herefordshire

Holly and beech

Day 67
25 May, 6.07 pm
SO 551 155
Wye Valley, Herefordshire

Ivy and rhododendron

Day 71
29 May, 4.39 pm
SH 743 226
Mawddach Valley, Gwynedd

River Mawddach

Day 71
29 May, 8.52 pm
SH 734 213
Gwynedd

Mawddach Estuary

Day 72
30 May, 6.42 am
SH 626 163
Gwynedd

River Wye

Day 76
3 June, 7.54 pm
SN 946 706
Powys

Dismantled railway bridge at Gamallt

Day 76
3 June, 8.23 pm
SN 947 706
Powys

Farmyard

Day 76
3 June, 9.59 pm
SO 010 671
Rhayader, Powys

Praa Sands

Day 78
5 June, 5.59 am
sw 576 281
Cornwall

Sorrell, cock's foot and common vetch

Day 80
7 June, 7.57 pm
SW 596 297
Cornwall

Above St Michael's Mount

Day 81
8 June, 7.25 am
SW 488 326
Cornwall

Near Logan's Rock

Day 86
13 June, 5.28 am
SW 397 220
Cornwall

Beside the Camel Estuary

Day 87
14 June, 6.02 am
sw 938 741
Cornwall

The Greenaway

Day 88
15 June, 8.12 pm
SW 929 785
Trebetherick, Cornwall

Reeds, cow parsley and burdock

Day 96
23 June, 4.56 am
ST 423 229
Thorney, Somerset

West Moor

Day 96
23 June, 5.01 am
ST 421 230
Thorney, Somerset

Midelney Pumping Station

Day 96
23 June, 5.16 am
ST 418 232
Thorney, Somerset

Barbury Down

Day 102
29 June, 5.12 am
SU 150 762
Wiltshire

Barbury Castle

Day 102
29 June, 5.27 am
SU 150 762
Marlborough Downs, Wiltshire

Marlborough Downs

Day 102
29 June, 6.17 am
SU 146 762
Wiltshire

Uffington Castle

Day 102
29 June, 11.41 am
SU 300 863
Oxfordshire

The Ridge Way

Day 102
29 June, 12.39 pm
SU 305 864
Oxfordshire

Golden Meadow from Duck Meadow

Day 105
2 July, 4.52 am
SU 564 345
Hampshire

Candover Brook

Day 105
2 July, 4.37 am
SU 564 345
Hampshire

Spring-fed side stream in Cottons

Day 105
2 July, 5.49 am
SU 564 345
Hampshire

Path on the big bend

Day 114
11 July, 8.49 pm
su 869 439
River Wey, Surrey

Poplars

Day 116
13 July, 5.02 am
SU 870 441
Tilhill, Surrey

Oaks

Day 116
13 July, 5.04 am
SU 870 441
Tilhill, Surrey

Alders

Day 117
14 July, 1.09 pm
SU 869 439
River Wey, Surrey

Riverbank

Day 118
15 July, 8.10 pm
SU 869 440
River Wey, Surrey

Beachy Head

Day 122
19 July, 4.18 pm
TV 571 953
East Sussex

Warningore Bostal

Day 127
24 July, 1.22 pm
TQ 372 126
East Sussex

Path below Black Cap

Day 127
24 July, 2.01 pm
TQ 378 130
East Sussex

The Lawns

Day 128
25 July, 4.25 am
TQ 456 102
Glyndebourne, East Sussex

The Brooks

Day 128
25 July, 5.21 am
TQ 460 111
Glyndebourne, East Sussex

Peartree Field

Day 128
25 July, 5.46 am
TQ 456 102
East Sussex

Firle Beacon from Mount Caburn

Day 128
25 July, 6.19 am
TQ 451 095
East Sussex

South Downs

Day 128
25 July, 8.11 pm
TQ 372 126
East Sussex

Beneath ash trees

Day 130
27 July, 3.34 pm
TQ 456 106
Glyndebourne, East Sussex

Sunlight through alders

Day 117
14 July, 12.37 pm
SU 869 439
River Wey, Surrey

Cuckmere Haven

Day 131
28 July, 6.30 am
TV 522 992
East Sussex

Seven Sisters

Day 131
28 July, 8.21 am
TV 548 962
East Sussex

Midday, Top Lake

Day 131
28 July, 12.15 pm
TQ 456 106
Glyndebourne, East Sussex

Track towards Firle Beacon

Day 131
28 July, 7.31 pm
TQ 490 060
Alciston, East Sussex

Wheat field

Day 131
28 July, 7.57 pm
TQ 492 061
Alciston, East Sussex

Barksore Marshes and the Isle of Grain

Day 136
2 August, 5.46 am
TQ 875 669
River Medway, Kent

Iken, River Alde

Day 139
5 August, 5.40 am
TM 403 566
Suffolk

Spring tide

Day 175
10 September, 7.14 am
TF 847 458
Burnham Overy Staithe, Norfolk

North, Ely Cathedral

Day 185
20 September, 6.21 pm
TL 547 796
Cambridgeshire

East, willow trees

Day 185
20 September, 6.25 pm
TL 547 796
Cambridgeshire

River Trent

Day 188
23 September, 7.08 am
SK 768 521
Farndon, Nottinghamshire

Hathersage

Day 190
25 September, 6.44 pm
SK 239 809
Derbyshire

Callow Bank

Day 191
26 September, 5.10 pm
SK 259 828
Hathersage, Derbyshire

Towards Hathersage and the Hope Valley

Day 197
2 October, 4.23 pm
SK 238 846
Derbyshire

Bamford Moor, towards Crook Hill

Day 197
2 October, 5.49 pm
SK 225 864
Derbyshire

Moon over the Three Squadrons
Day 199
4 October, 6.32 pm
NY 496 229
Lowther, Cumbria

Calver Hill

Day 203
8 October, 4.22 pm
NZ 044 002
Arkengarthdale, North Yorkshire

Solway Firth, west

Day 206
11 October, 8.29 am
NY 057 642
Dumfries and Galloway

Daer Water

Day 206
11 October, 6.18 pm
NS 958 155
Lowther Hills, South Lanarkshire

Aonach Dubh

Day 207
12 October, 8.30 am
NN 170 568
Glen Coe, Highland

Loch Coruisk

Day 209
14 October, 3.36 pm
NG 491 197
Cuillin Hills, Isle of Skye

Technical note

The camera is a 10 × 8-inch view camera made of brass and wood. It has always seemed to me the perfect tool for taking photographs because it can take in more than I can see at the time. Each photograph is therefore full of details and relationships that emerge the more you look at the picture.

The camera is quite big, of course, but that's a good thing, as it begins to take on an important role in the landscape. I use a very heavy studio tripod, which balances the camera well on the shoulder. It's important that it all sits very firmly on the ground, but I often find that the camera is positioned unusually; in a river perhaps, on a steep slope or in the mud. I sometimes carry the camera quite far, but mostly what I am looking for is much closer to the van than I had expected.

I carry about six sheets of film in a medium-sized rucksack and use it sparingly, trying to take only one sheet of each scene. I took 350 sheets on this journey, and there were plenty of days and many ventures when I took no pictures. I also carry a spot meter for accurate light readings and a notebook for recording all the other information, such as sounds, wind direction, state of the tide and the general feel of the place. I have a small screwdriver for tightening up the camera, and a spare cable release. I don't use a darkcloth for focusing on the screen, but instead use the coat I am wearing at the time. If it's cold, I take a woollen blanket to cover the camera; and if it's wet, then I cover it in a large canoeing holdall. It doesn't matter too much if the camera gets wet, but the film, of course, must stay immaculate.

I use a 240 mm lens, which is a medium-wide-angle that takes in what you could call the natural sweep of one's vision. It allows for a natural relationship between the foreground and background that conveys as far as possible the experience of being there. On rare occasions I use a slightly wider 210 mm lens, if I am unable to get far enough away from what I am photographing; however, I generally prefer the consistency of using a single lens.

The lens stops down to an aperture of f64, which allows for the whole scene to be in focus; a great depth of field. Sometimes, however, this is not possible, such as when it's getting dark or at dawn, when a small aperture

Shetland Islands

Shetland Islands

South Downs

Cornwall

North Uist

Wye Valley

Cornwall

Teesdale

Teesdale

River Trent

Isle of Skye

Isle of Skye

would require an exposure of perhaps more than ten minutes. This can often create some extraordinary results, but it begins to abstract the image photographically and distract from the experience of being there. For me, it is important that the photograph looks and feels as it did at the time.

I work from a van that has a cooler to hold the film, a small gas burner for cooking and a bed. There's a place to attach the tripod, and I have a battery to power the laptop and a few wooden boxes to stop everything rattling around. The tailgate opens up to provide shelter when it's raining.

I use negative colour film rated at 160 ASA. I send batches of about thirty sheets back to Jean Lippett at Visions in London to be processed, and she then makes two contact sheets from each negative: one for me and one for herself. I try to wait as long as possible before choosing which print to enlarge, and it is often more than a year before I ask Jean to work her magic and make a print. The first prints we produce are 20 × 16 inches, as it is only at this size that you begin to see the detail within.

I use ten darkslides that take a total of twenty sheets of film. I therefore have to change film about once a week in a light-tight changing bag. I never do this in the van because it is cramped and dusty, but find use of a large table, usually in a restaurant or café when no one else is around.

Index

Published by Merrell Publishers Limited

81 Southwark Street
London SE1 0HX

merrellpublishers.com

First published 2007
Paperback edition first published 2009

British Library Cataloguing-in-Publication Data:
Wright, Harry Cory
Journey through the British Isles
1. Wright, Harry Cory – Travel – Great Britain
2. Landscape – Great Britain – Pictorial works
3. Great Britain – Pictorial works
4. Great Britain – Description and travel
I. Title
779.3′6′41

ISBN 978-1-8589-4480-7

Produced by Merrell Publishers Limited
Designed by Nicola Bailey
Copy-edited by Mary Scott
Proof-read by Barbara Roby
Indexed by Hilary Bird
Printed and bound in China

FRONT COVER
Beachy Head, East Sussex, see p. 135

BACK COVER, LEFT TO RIGHT
Lund, Unst, Shetland Islands, see p. 23; Holly and beech, Wye Valley, Herefordshire, see p. 81; Firle Beacon from Mount Caburn, East Sussex, see p. 143

PAGE 2
Candover Brook from Duck Meadow
Day 105
2 July, 5.04 am
SU 564 345
Hampshire

PAGE 4
Scaleber, Settle
Day 62
20 May, 8.49 pm
SD 845 627
North Yorkshire

PAGE 7, TOP TO BOTTOM
Balta from the Keen of Hamar, Unst, Shetland Islands, see p. 25
Loch Druim Suardalain and Quinag, Sutherland, see p. 39
Beside the River Tees, Teesdale, County Durham, see p. 67
Firle Beacon from Mount Caburn, East Sussex, see p. 143
Bamford Moor, towards Crook Hill, Derbyshire, see p. 175

PAGE 8, TOP TO BOTTOM
Ben Loyal and Ben Hope, Sutherland, see p. 33
Path to Castle Crag, Borrowdale, Cumbria, see p. 63
Sorrell, cock's foot and common vetch, Cornwall, see p. 96
Sunlight through alders, River Wey, Surrey, see p. 147
Loch Coruisk, Cuillin Hills, Isle of Skye, see p. 187

HARRY CORY WRIGHT is a leading British landscape photographer. In 1998 he began to document the coastlines of Britain and Ireland through large colour photographs. Cory Wright set up the publishing company Saltwater Books in 2000, and the Saltwater Gallery in 2001. He lives in Norfolk with his family.

ADAM NICOLSON is the author of many books on travel, history and the environment, among them *Sea Room* (2001), *Seamanship* (2004), *Men of Honour* (2005), *Earls of Paradise* (2008) and *Sissinghurst: An Unfinished History* (2008). He has won several awards for his writing, including the Somerset Maugham Award, the British Topography Prize and the Royal Society of Literature's William Heinemann Prize. He lives with his family at Sissinghurst Castle in Kent.

All photographs for sale in two sizes:

200 x 160 cm limited edition of 3
100 x 80 cm limited edition of 7

For further information, see journeythroughthebritishisles.com